Dance to your own
mooooosic !!.
Cheryl Kirking ♪

To everyone, young and old, who dances to their own beat!
To my parents. LeVerne and Jean Kirking, who raised me on a farm,
To David, Blake, Sarah Jean and Bryce for playing and dancing along the way.
—C.K.

To my mother, father, and sister who have believed in me,
and encouraged me to never give up on my dreams.
—J.J.

Text and music copyright © 2012 by Cheryl Kirking

Illustrations copyright 2012 by Jason Jolda

The audio recording *Evangeline the Dancing Holstein* originally copyright ©1995 by Cheryl Kirking from the CD *Get Moovin'!*

 Mill House Press, P.O. Box 525, Lake Mills, Wisconsin 53551 USA www.millhousepress.com

Book design: Jonathan Gullery

ISBN: 978-0-578-06055-2

Library of Congress Cataloging-in-Publication Data

Kirking, Cheryl

Evangeline the Dancing Holstein/Cheryl Kirking; illustrated by Jason Jolda

Summary: Evangeline the dancing cow leads the noisy, musical fun after the farmer leaves the barn for the night.

1. Farm life-fiction. 2. Stories in Rhyme-fiction 3. Domestic animals-fiction. 4. Dancing-fiction.

For library and school visits, writer's workshops, and concerts, please contact the author at www.cherylkirking.com or the publisher at www.millhousepress.com.

For free reproducible coloring pages and activities to enjoy along with this book, please visit www.millhousepress.com

Manufactured in the United States.

CPSIA Compliance Information: Batch # 1109
For further information contact
RJ Communications, NY NY,
800-621-2556

EVANGELINE!
the Dancing Holstein

Mill House Press

by **Cheryl Kirking** with illustrations by Jason Jolda

And the farmer turns out the light

As the door shuts behind him
and his footsteps fade

The animals get set for the night!

The cat turns on the radio,
the dog gets the light

The cows start to sway to the beat.

And a certain bovine who dances so fine
Smiles and rises to her dainty hooved feet.

She's Evangeline,
she's a cool Holstein!

Evangeline, she's a dance machine!

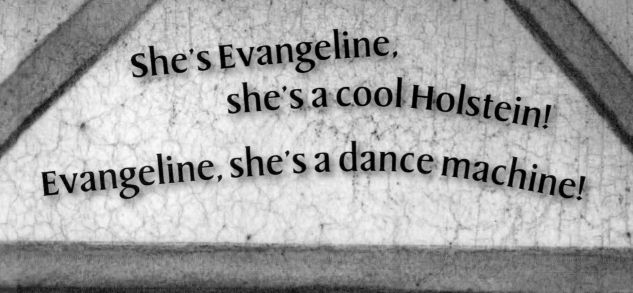

She can rock, she can roll
she can boogie with soul,

EVANGELINE!

Well, Lucy the Goose

starts to shake her caboose

And Rover keeps time with his tail.

Mule keeps the beat by stomping his feet,

And Piggy drums on an old pail.

The cows are really hoofin' as they romp in the aisle

Its 2:00am in the barn on the hill

And the animals call it a night.

The cat turns off the radio
And Rover turns out the light

The cows settle down as they drift off to sleep.

All is quiet
it seems...

She's dancing still in her dreams!

She can rock, she can roll, she can boogie with soul,

EVANGELINE!

EVANGELINE!

Riddles

1. How do you describe a grumpy cow?

2. What animals do you walk with wherever you go?

3. What do you call a sleeping bull?

4. What do cows like to dance to?

(answers on the next page)

Knock Knock!
Who's there?
Cows
Cows who?
No, owls "who." Cows go "moo!"

For more downloadable activities related to this book, visit

www.millhousepress.com.

Did you know?

- Cows have very flexible ears that can turn in any direction in order to hear better.
- Cows eat grass, hay, corn, and other types of plants.
- Cows are female, bulls are male, and the babies are called calves. Together they are all known as "cattle." A large group of cattle is called a *herd*.
- A grown *Holstein* cow weighs about 1400 pounds and stands about 58" at the shoulder.

- All *bovines* have *cloven* hooves. This means there is a split (or cleft) in the hooves, which allows the toes to spread. This is helpful when they walk in deep mud or boggy places, as the wider foot keeps them from sinking in the mud. Horses have solid hooves and cannot walk as well in mud as cows.
- Dairy cows are raised to produce milk. *Holsteins* are a breed of cow known for their black and white spots.

- Cows sleep lying down, although many people mistakenly believe they sleep standing up, as horses often do.
- Cows are *bovines*. A *bovine* is an animal which belongs to the biological subfamily known as Bovinae. Cattle, buffalo, bison, oxen and the yak all belong to the *Bovine* family, as well as four-horned and spiral-horned antelope.

CHERYL KIRKING is a songwriter and award-winning author of seven books and six CDs of original songs for children and grownups. She grew up on a dairy farm and graduated from the University of Wisconsin-Madison in education with graduate studies in counseling and guidance. A former classroom teacher and concert artist, she develops musical character education programs for schools, and entertains audiences of all ages with her Ripples of Encouragement™ Keynotes and Concerts. To learn more about her books, CDs and concerts, visit www.cherylkirking.com

JASON JOLDA graduated from the Columbus College of Art and Design with a BFA in Illustration and furthered his education at the Savannah College of Art and Design to pursue his MFA in Visual Communication. He has freelanced for advertising agencies, private businesses and individual clients and has taught drawing at the Maine College of Art and York County Community college in southern Maine. Jason is known for his unique layering technique in which he incorporates a variety of traditional mediums to create rich textures, playing up light and shadow.

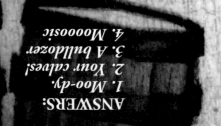

ANSWERS:
1. Moo-dy.
2. Your calves!
3. A bulldozer
4. Moooosic